$\mathcal{P}$resented to:

$\mathcal{F}$rom:

$\mathcal{D}$ate:

The Desperate Husband's Guide

101 Ways to Say "I Love You"

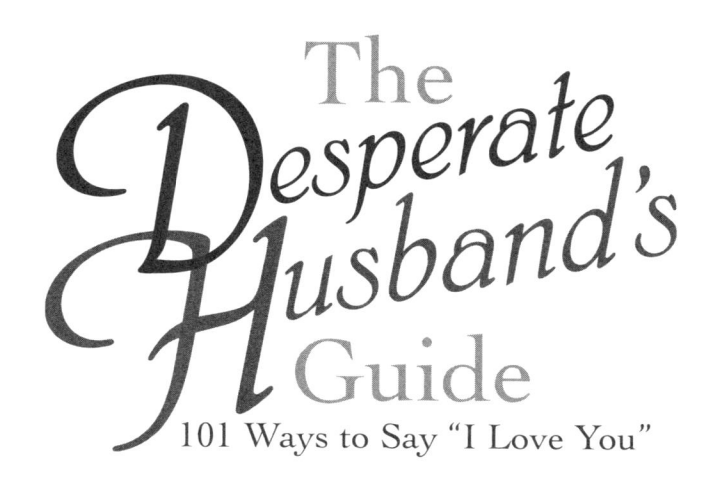

HONOR BOOKS

Inspiration and Motivation for the Seasons of Life

COOK COMMUNICATIONS MINISTRIES
Colorado Springs, Colorado • Paris, Ontario
KINGSWAY COMMUNICATIONS LTD
Eastbourne, England

Honor® is an imprint of
Cook Communications Ministries, Colorado Springs, CO 80918
Cook Communications, Paris, Ontario
Kingsway Communications, Eastbourne, England

THE DESPERATE HUSBAND'S GUIDE: 101 WAYS TO SAY "I LOVE YOU"
© 2006 by Honor Books

All rights reserved. No part of this book may be reproduced without written permission, except for brief quotations in books and critical reviews. For information, write Cook Communications Ministries, 4050 Lee Vance View, Colorado Springs, CO 80918.

Manuscript written by Dan Benson

Cover Design: Ryan Putman/BMB Design

First Printing, 2006
Printed in the United States of America

1 2 3 4 5 6 7 8 9 10 Printing/Year 10 09 08 07 06

Scripture quotations marked NLT are taken from the Holy Bible, New Living Translation, copyright © 1996. Used by permission of Tyndale House Publishers, Inc., Wheaton, Illinois 60189. All rights reserved. Scripture quotations marked KJV are taken from the King James Version of the Bible. (Public Domain.) Italics in Scripture quotations are added by the author for emphasis.

ISBN 1-56292-745-0

des·per·ate *adj*: characterized by a dazed, deer-in-headlights countenance among men everywhere upon sudden realization that today is her birthday, their wedding anniversary, Valentine's Day, or simply that he's in trouble. Observed most frequently in the greeting card or jewelry counter.

hus·band *noun*: two-legged carnivore often afflicted with above condition. Realizes he used his best stuff to get her to marry him and now stumbles about mumbling, "What do I do now?"

> "Love sought is good, but given unsought is better."
>
> William Shakespeare
> *Twelfth Night*

Desperate husbands, the bard speaketh wisely.

The love of which Shakespeare writes is romance, a word that warms the hearts of women and curdles the blood of men. In this perceptive line, the playwright underscores the joy of a romantic love that flows naturally, spontaneously—without manipulation or coercion.

Unfortunately, such romantic joy has departed from far too many marriages. And, gentlemen, can we be honest here? Many of us are to blame.

Why is it that, after a passionate courtship and honeymoon, we often let the princely courtesies, romantic gifts, and magic moments become buried by routine?

Possibly it's because familiarity breeds complacency. When the thrill of the chase is over, when we discover that the other hangs the toilet paper backward, when wet screaming little bundles of joy enter the picture, the passion fires start to die. Complacency, if unchecked, becomes boredom.

That's why the wedding should not signal the end of the courtship, but the beginning.

You hold in your hands 101 proven ideas to help you be creative in saying "I Love You" to your wife. Choose and use one idea in the next couple of days. When she recovers from shock, put another in motion. Don't be surprised if she asks, "Who are you and what have you done with my husband?" Just smile and rekindle the romantic adventure. From there, try one idea each week to keep the flames going. And ... have fun!

101 Ways to Say "I Love You" to Your Wife

1

Leave a love note for her—around the house, in her car, in her purse or briefcase.

2

Ask her for a date on Friday night, and arrange for a babysitter. When you're dressed, slip out of the house and come to the door for her, flowers in hand.

3

$\mathcal{G}$et gourmet coffee and breakfast pastries and watch the sunrise together.

4

Phone her during the day just to tell her how much you love and appreciate her. No business talk allowed.

5

*T*ell her, "You're my best friend"
—and mean it.

6

$\mathcal{G}$ive her a back rub without being asked.

7

Laugh at her jokes.

8

Plan a "World's Greatest Mom" dinner with the kids. Have them make a trophy, banner, decorations, the works—including testimonials on why their mother is the world's greatest mom. Pitch in with your own testimonial, too!

9

*M*ake her a Valentine —
any day of the year.

10

Follow this guideline in your house: "I won't sit down till she can sit down." In other words, make kitchen work and housework a shared responsibility, a partnership. Use this work time together for conversation, jokes, even play.

11

Write her a poem expressing your feelings about something intimate between the two of you. A warm memory. A recent walk together. An argument that, when settled, helped draw you closer together. The beauty, love, skill you observe in her.

12

Surprise her with breakfast in bed. And not just on her birthday or Mother's Day. If she asks, "What's the occasion?" as you fluff her pillows behind her, just smile and say, "No particular reason ...
I just love you."

13

Warm her side of the bed before she gets in.

"Love is that condition in which the happiness of another person is essential to your own."

Robert A. Heinlein
Stranger in a Strange Land

14

$\mathcal{B}$ring home a pint of her favorite ice cream. Pick a good moment later in the evening, have her sit and relax, and serve her.

15

Buy a box of large gelatin capsules at your pharmacy. Count out fifty-two capsules and on a sheet of paper write fifty-two promissory one-liners such as:

- One movie of your choice with yours truly
- Three consecutive nights of total freedom from kitchen duties
- One pizza with the works on the evening of your choice
- One long walk together
- One leisurely breakfast out together
- One new blouse of your choice
- One sexy new outfit (of my choice)

$\mathcal{S}$ome may require money, others merely time and attention, but each will be a special treat for her — something she can claim from you anytime. Take a pair of scissors to the sheet, then roll up each note and insert one into each capsule.

Now find an old prescription bottle and make a label that reads: "Rx from Dr. [your name] for [her name]. To prevent dull marriage, take one capsule every week for the next year." Half the fun will be watching her continually fight off the urge to open them all at once.

16

$\mathcal{S}$ay, "Honey, I need your advice."
(Then listen.)

17

*C*hoose and read a book together.

18

Accept her folks, warts and all. Take initiative to show and tell them you love them.

19

Give her frequent "space" breaks—opportunities to get away from you, the house, the children, her job ... and blow off steam. Fill the tank of her car with gas and tell her you'll watch the kids. Her only responsibility for the day is to go out and have fun.

20

Phone her at home or at her job and arrange to meet during the day for lunch. Use this time to talk about your life together, plans for the family and the future, or anything that's on her mind.

21

Serve her during mealtime. Many wives, and most mothers, are forced to eat their food cold because they are constantly hopping up from the table to serve everyone's needs. Let her sit and enjoy the food for once while you get another napkin for Junior or more iced tea for yourself. Teach your kids to practice this servant spirit also.

22

Kiss her passionately in front of the kids. (Enjoy the gasps of "yuck!" and "gross!")

23

Make a card with a love acrostic of her name. Conclude with this line: "Just a few reasons why I love you."

So ought men to love their wives as their own bodies. He that loveth his wife loveth himself.

Ephesians 5:28 KJV

24

Some Saturday morning, or a weekday if you can arrange it, write on a slip of paper: "Let's go to the amusement park today—just you and me," or "Let's go to the beach—just the two of us." Gift wrap it and present it to her with a kiss at breakfast.

25

When the two of you are at a party or gathering, catch her eye with a wink and a smile. Let her know that of all the women in the room, she's the most attractive and important to you.

26

At the same gathering, take her hand and whisper in her ear, "I can't wait to get you home...." She may feign embarrassment, but she'll love it.

27

Never, ever compare her to old girlfriends, Mom, Sis, or anyone else. Revel in her uniqueness!

28

Keep her car serviced and fueled for her.

29

Make the bed in the morning while she's in the bathroom or fixing breakfast.

30

Send her a singing telegram. (Better yet, do the singing telegram yourself. Sneak outside, ring the front doorbell, and prepare to be laughed at ... or hauled away.)

31

Take the initiative to pray together. Nothing will give her greater security than knowing you are totally dedicated to God and his guidance. Go to him together in thanks, in praise, in problem solving.

32

As you pray together, take her hand and thank God for giving her to you. If you sneak a peek (go ahead, the Lord won't mind), you'll probably catch her smiling.

33

Make it a policy never to speak negatively of her to another person — in her presence or in her absence. It's all about trust — she needs to know without a doubt that she can trust you with her faults and eccentricities, just as you trust her with yours.

34

From the next room, call out, "Honey?" When she responds, just say, "I love you." (This tells her you're thinking good thoughts about her.)

35

Remember the partnership. Be alert for all the things you can do to keep your home running smoothly and make things easier on her. If you finish the orange juice, mix a new batch. Replace the empty toiletpaper roll (hanging end outside, or whatever she prefers). Sweep down a cobweb. Take on the vacuuming.

36
Feed the dog.

37
Feed the baby.

38
Change the diapers (on the baby).

39

If Junior has discovered the trick of bawling for Mommy late at night, let Mom rest. She's earned it. Tend to him yourself.

40

Three surprises that'll be like a breath of fresh air to her:

- "Let's go out to dinner."
- "Let's go buy you a new _____ [item of clothing]."
- "Let's go away for the weekend — just the two of us."

41

Check in daily with 1 Corinthians 13, the Bible's classic "love chapter." How would your wife rate you in the following areas?

- Love is patient and kind.
- Love is not jealous or boastful or proud or rude.
- Love does not demand its own way.
- Love is not irritable, and it keeps no record of when it has been wronged.
- Love never gives up, never loses faith, is always hopeful, and endures through every circumstance (NLT).

42

Drive or walk together to a good vantage point and admire a sunset.

43

If she's on a diet or fitness binge, encourage her. Fat jokes are definitely out. If you see improvement, however slight, be sure to tell her. "Honey, you're looking better and better," will bring a smile and renewed determination on her part. (And while she's at it, why not join her?)

Nurturing your relationship means keeping it current, warm, juicy, sparkling with gratitude, burnished with respect.... It is the act of creating an environment in which the relationship, and each person, flourish.

Jennifer Louden
The Couple's Comfort Book

44

Purchase a car emergency kit for her car and give her an auto club membership. If she doesn't have a cell phone, get her one.

45

$\mathcal{S}$ay, "I really enjoy being with you."

46

Tell your children often how much you love their mother. Then let them see it in action every day. If you treat her like a queen, chances are they'll do so too.

47

Scheme with the kids on creative ways to surprise Mom:

- Plan and prepare a meal.
- Clean the house while she's gone.
- Make a special gift for her.
- Plan a "Queen for a Day" celebration.

48

Turn the phones off before and during family meals and during intimate times in the bedroom.

To keep your marriage brimming
With love in the loving cup,
When you're wrong, admit it.
When you're right, shut up.

Ogden Nash

49

Never let hand-holding become a thing of the past. It's one of those little things she'll never grow tired of. In sitting or walking together, take her hand proudly. Exception (learned the hard way): Avoid the above when she's painting her nails.

50

Ask her perspective on a current event. Encourage her to elaborate. Show her you value her insight and opinion.

51

Be adventurous! Try new restaurants. Explore new pathways or resort towns. Pick a new recreational activity and go for it.

52

$\mathcal{C}$ompliment her.

53

Show interest in her activities and work. Ask questions to show you really want to know her world better.

54

$\mathcal{B}$irthdays and anniversaries, of course, are special occasions and should always be commemorated as such. (Write them on your personal calendar at the start of every year.) But try these little surprises for "no special occasion":

- a single long-stemmed rose
- a bouquet or plant delivered to her at her work place or at home
- a slinky nightgown (shopping for it is half the fun)
- a CD of her favorite musician
- a DVD of her favorite chick flick
- a video she's been wanting to see
- a scented candle or potpourri
- a helium-filled balloon
- a perfume she likes
- a romantic or humorous greeting card
- a craft or jigsaw puzzle that you, she, and the kids can work on together
- a ring, necklace, earrings, or bracelet
- a book she's been wanting to read
- a new photo of you and/or the kids

55

*E*ven better, surprise her with something you've made yourself:

- a plaque
- a sculpture or pottery
- a painting
- a greeting card with original poetry and artwork
- a scented candle
- a framed photograph of a memorable scene or cute animal*

*We realize the word "cute" is not part of the desperate husband's vocabulary, but bear with us. We're trying to help here.

56

When it comes to Christmas, birthdays, or anniversaries, forget the practical stuff. Don't even think about a new toaster or iron. Those are household items, not love gifts. (Would you have bought her such things when you were dating her?) Use these times of the year to find the creative little extravagances that tell her she's well worth a splurge.

If you cannot inspire a woman with love of you, fill her above the brim with love of herself— all that runs over will be yours.

Charles Caleb Colton
Lacon

57

$\mathcal{P}$hone her when you're delayed in coming home from work.

58

Give her a big, unhurried hug.

59

Leave the toilet seat down when you leave the bathroom.

60

$\mathcal{G}$et her consent well in advance of inviting a friend home to dinner.
(Rule: Ask, don't tell.)

61

*S*ay, "You're sure a good lover."

62

In your mutual financial planning, allot her a personal spending allowance equal to (or greater than) your own, to do with as she chooses.

63

Make sure you have an up-to-date will, living will, and durable power of attorney as well as adequate life, medical, and disability insurance to provide for her and the kids if, as insurance agents are trained to say, "something should happen to you."

We should measure affection, not like youngsters by the ardor of its passion, but by its strength and constancy.

Marcus Tullius Cicero
De Officiis

64

Organize a notebook for her that explains where all the essential family records are located (mortgage, insurance policies, tax and investment records) and whom to contact if something should happen to you.

65

$\mathcal{G}$ive her a foot rub.

66

Take the kids to breakfast or their morning activities and let her sleep in.

67

Renew your wedding vows ... and make it a surprise. While on a quiet date, propose to her all over again, complete with ring and flowers. Prearrange for your minister and a few close friends to show up on cue and (assuming she accepts) redo your wedding vows then and there.

68

When you both arrive home at the end of the workday, search her out and give her a big, prolonged hug first thing. Show her that seeing her is the best part of your day.

69

Set aside at least some quality minutes each day just to visit with her. Make it a time when the kids are busy or in bed, when chores are over and you're both starting to unwind from the day. Turn the phones off and talk together about the things on each other's minds ... about goals ... about dreams. Make a special effort to listen to, encourage, and affirm this special woman God has given you.

70

When watching TV together, let her have the remote control … for the entire viewing time. (We realize this is totally unnatural for the male species, so keep a Valium handy.)

71

Admire her wisdom and intelligence.

72

If you must leave town on business, hide little love treasures around the house for her to discover:

- a romantic card under her pillow
- a chocolate truffle on her desk
- a single flower in a vase
- a bookmark in her Bible
- a love note propped in front of her dressing mirror.

Woman was created from the rib of man. She was not made from his head, to top him; nor from his feet, to be trampled on. She was made from his side, to be equal to him; from under his arm, to be protected by him; from near his heart, to be loved by him.

Author Unknown

73

Sing her praises! Tell others what you appreciate about her. Go beyond physical attributes and practical skills — praise her character qualities as well.

74

True, a home is to be lived in, but slobdom has no place in ongoing courtship. And let's face it, the way we desperate husbands dress and behave at home can be as romantic to her as boogers on toast. Pay some attention to your appearance and manners, just as you did when you were dating her.

75

*H*ire a plane to tow a love message over a public gathering.

76

If she asks, "Does this make me look fat?" there is only one correct answer. And that answer determines where you sleep tonight.

77

$\mathcal{I}$n a group discussion, ask, "What do you think, Hon?"

78

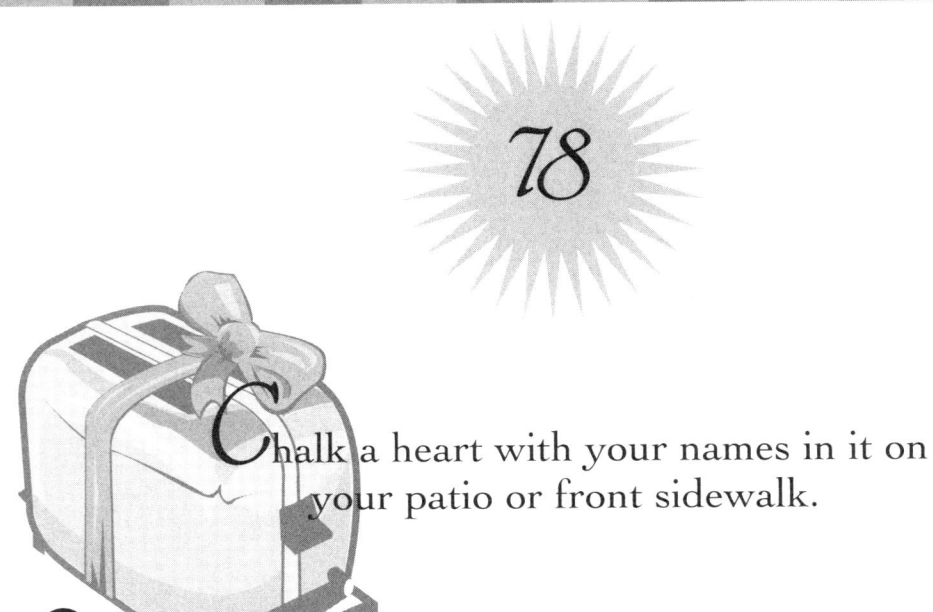

Chalk a heart with your names in it on your patio or front sidewalk.

79

Try to accompany her when she goes grocery shopping. Or do the shopping yourself.

You husbands must love your wives with the same love Christ showed the church.

Ephesians 5:25 NLT

80

Give her a gift certificate for a lesson or class she's always wanted to take.

81

Express appreciation for the contribution she makes around the house. Notice the rooms that are straightened and vacuumed, your ironed shirts, the aroma of what's cooking. Compliment and thank her as you give her a warm hug. Never take her hard work for granted.
(Coach the kids on this one too!)

82

Three statements she'll never grow tired of hearing:
"You sure are looking good today."
"I'm sure glad you're my wife."
"You're my favorite person in the whole world."

83

Tell her parents how much you love their daughter. Thank them for the great job they did raising her and for letting you marry her.

84

Help her prepare dinner and clean up afterward. Train the kids to participate too.

Give honor to marriage, and remain faithful to one another in marriage. God will surely judge people who are immoral and those who commit adultery.

Hebrews 13:4 NLT

85

Watch for the smile in her eyes when you dust off some of those "manners" that desperate husbands tend to abandon shortly after the I dos:

- Open her car door for her (even if she's the driver).
- At the dinner table and in restaurants, hold her chair for her. After she's seated, give her a kiss on the cheek and whisper, "I love you."
- Open doors for her (and, yes, let her enter first).
- While walking with her, walk on the most hazardous side.

86

$\mathcal{E}$mpty the trash without her having to ask.

87

$\mathcal{S}$urprise her with some extra "mad money" for the week.

88

Remember those pesky fixes and repairs she's been mentioning? Grab the tools and do one or two tonight. Then complete the rest this weekend.

89

$\mathcal{L}$et her know that her phone calls are always welcome while you're at the office.

90

If you haven't done so already, abandon the old male habit of making wisecracks about the intelligence of women, women drivers, women talkers, women shoppers. She's a woman, and these baseless slurs are also a slur on her.*

*And, hey, if she makes a man-joke at your expense, don't retaliate. Women owe us, big-time. They've endured decades of our put-downs and now we must shut up and take our medicine.

91

*H*elp her keep the family correspondence going.

> "They do not love
> that do not show
> their love."
>
> William Shakespeare
> *Two Gentlemen of Verona*

92

Compliment her mothering skills. Thank her for all she does as your kids' mom.

93

Memorize Galatians 5:22–23, the apostle Paul's recitation of the "fruit of the Spirit." Each day, ask God to help you exercise these nine character qualities as a husband and father. (And from time to time, ask her to tell you how you're doing with each one!)

- Love
- Joy
- Peace
- Patience
- Kindness
- Goodness
- Faithfulness
- Gentleness
- Self-control

94

Select a scenic spot in the park, prepare a gourmet picnic complete with her favorite wine or beverage, and tell her to reserve two hours and "dress casual." (If, like many desperate husbands, you are culinarily challenged, check the yellow pages for a shop that will prepare a portable feast for you.) Give her your full, relaxed attention as the two of you enjoy this special time together.

95

Make idea 94 even more special by adding a flair or two:

- Slip a small volume of love poems in the picnic basket. During or after the meal, pull it out and read several poems to her.
- Arrange for a special delivery of flowers, balloons, or her favorite gourmet coffee and a chocolate truffle.
- Have a violinist, classic guitarist, or barbershop quartet drop by to serenade the two of you with love songs.

96

$\mathcal{T}$ake a ballroom dancing class together.

> *When you love you wish to do things for. You wish to sacrifice for. You wish to serve."*
>
> Ernest Hemingway
> *A Farewell to Arms*

97

Bring flowers home to her. No special occasion, and not because you've blown it. Just to say, "I love you."

98

Read to each other from Psalms and reflect together on God's enduring majesty, love, and provision.

99

$\mathcal{T}$ake a leisurely stroll together in the rain or snow.

> *Life has taught us that love does not consist of gazing at each other but in looking outward together in the same direction.*
>
> Antoine de Saint-Exupéry
> *Wind, Sand, and Stars*

100

$\mathcal{T}$ake initiative to dream together. What fun and worthwhile things would you both like to do in the next ten years? Once the nest is empty? In your senior years?

101

Never let a day go by without saying "I love you."

Never Quit Courting

To keep your married love fun and fulfilling, never let the courtship end. Keep romancing your special lady as if you were trying to win her for the very first time.

Gradually, you'll notice that your love and admiration for her are growing even stronger. And hers for you. There'll be a new liveliness to your interaction, a new sense of adventure to your relationship. You'll almost feel like you're honeymooning again—only now your love and respect for each other will be greater than ever.

*If you'd be loved,
be worthy
to be loved.*

Ovid
The Art of Love

Other portables available from Honor Books:

Happy Valentine's Day

100 Hints: How to Stay Married for Life

Relationships 101

Sweet Smarts for Sweethearts

The Simply Romantic Husband

Additional copies of this
and other Honor products are available
wherever good books are sold.

If you have enjoyed this book,
or if it has had an impact on your life,
we would like to hear from you.

Please contact us at:

Honor Books
Cook Communications Ministries, Dept. 201
4050 Lee Vance View
Colorado Springs, CO 80918
Or visit our Web site: www.cookministries.com

HONOR BOOKS